A
Shit.., ...

by Katherine Chandler

Created from an original idea
by Francesca Goodridge and
Katherine Chandler

||SAMUEL FRENCH||

FOR AMATEUR PRODUCTION ENQUIRIES

UNITED KINGDOM AND WORLD
EXCLUDING NORTH AMERICA
licensing@concordtheatricals.co.uk
020-7054-7298

Each title is subject to availability from Concord Theatricals,
depending upon country of performance.

USE OF COPYRIGHTED MUSIC

USE OF COPYRIGHTED THIRD-PARTY MATERIALS

IMPORTANT BILLING AND CREDIT REQUIREMENTS

A PRETTY SHITTY LOVE was first produced at Theatr Clwyd on Friday 8th July 2022. The cast was as follows:

HAYLEY . . . . .Danielle Bird
CARL . . . . Daniel Hawksford

Writer – Katherine Chandler
Director – Francesca Goodridge
Designer – Lulu Tam
Lighting Designer – Jess Bernberg
Composer and Sound Designer – Alexandra Faye Braithwaite
Video Designer – Libby Ward
Movement Director – Yandass Ndlovu
Casting Director – Polly Jerrold
Assistant Director – Amy Roberts
Company Stage Manager – Harriet Stewart
Deputy Stage Manager – Natasha Guzel
Stage Management Placement – Emma Hardwick
Producer – Ric Watts
Production Manager – Jim Davis
Head of Production – Hannah Lobb
Technical Manager – Geoff Farmer
Senior Technician (Lighting) – Chris Skinner
Senior Technician (Stage) – Nic Samuel
Senior Technician (Sound & AV) – Matthew Williams
Wardrobe Manager – Debbie Knight
Workshop Manager – Steve Eccleson
Workshop Deputy - Rob Wilson
Scenic Artist – Katy Salt
WHAM Consultant - Lindy Davies

CAST

DANIELLE BIRD | HAYLEY

Theatre credits include: *The Comedy Of Errors* (Mercury Theatre, Colchester); *Beauty and The Beast* (New Vic Theatre); *Charlie & Stan Tour* (Told By An Idiot); *The Comedy of Errors* (Storyhouse Theatre); *The Prince and The Pauper* (New Victoria Theatre); *The Worst Witch* (Vaudeville Theatre); *Astley's Astounding Adventures* (New Victoria Theatre Newcastle); *Aladdin* (Theatre Royal, Wakefield); *The Hypocrite* (Hull Truck/Royal Shakespeare Company); *Macbeth* (Shakespeare's Globe Theatre); *NotMoses* (Arts Theatre); *The Lion, The Witch and The Wardrobe* (Birmingham REP); *Alice's Adventures Underground* (Les Enfants Terribles); *Comedy of Errors, Macbeth, A Midsummer Night's Dream, Othello* and *Cyrano De Bergerac* (Chester Performs/Grosvenor Open Air Theatre); *Princess and The Pea* (York Theatre Royal); *Father Christmas and The Icicle Bicycle, Tea Time* (Oxford Playhouse); *The Prince and The Pauper* (Unicorn Theatre); *Colin Hoult's Real Horror Show* (Leicester Square Theatre); *No Ball Games* (New Wolsey Theatre); *As You Like It* (Principal Theatre); *Slick* (Scarabeus Theatre Dance Company); *Romeo and Juliet, Hamlet* (Young Shakespeare Company); *Magician's Assistant* (You Me Bum Bum Train). Danielle also performs stilt walking, puppetry and storytelling shows with the circus theatre company Circo Rum Ba Ba.

Television credits include: *Hapless* (Netflix), *Vengeance* (Light Films), *The Investigator* (ITV/Netflix), *The Wives Did It* (Discovery), *Holby City* (BBC) and *The Double Life of Morton Coyle* (The Comedy Unit/BBC).

Film credits include: *Now You See Me 2* (Lionsgate), *A Running Jump*, Mike Leigh's Olympic film (BBC Films/Film4).

DANIEL HAWKSFORD | CARL

Theatre credits include: *Troilus and Cressida* (Royal Shakespeare Company); *Swansea's Three Day Blitz* (Grand Theatre Swansea); *Crouch, Touch, Pause, Engage* (National Theatre of Wales / Out of Joint); *ILLIAD* (National Theatre of Wales); *The Distance (Revival)* (Sheffield Crucible / Orange Tree Theatre); *Arms and the Man* (Theatr Clwyd); *The Distance* (Orange Tree Theatre); *Praxis Makes Perfect* (National Theatre Wales and Neon Neon); *Macbeth* (Pontardawe Arts Centre); *Macbeth* (Globe Theatre); *The Bible* (Globe Theatre); *The Dark Philosophers* (National Theatre Wales / Told by an Idiot); *Dancng at Lughnasa* (Birmingham Rep); *Judgement Day* (Almedia Theatre); *King Lear* (Globe Theatre); *Memory* (Theatr Clwyd / Pleasance Theatre). *Much Ado About Nothing, The Hour We Knew Nothing Of Each Other* (National Theatre); *Jackets* (Young Vic/Theatre 503); *Troilus and Cressida* (Theatr Clwyd); *The Taming of The Shrew, Cymbeline, The School of Night, The Tamer Tamed* (Royal Shakespeare Company); *Romeo and Juliet, Rosencrantz and Guildenstern Are Dead* (Theatr Clwyd).

Television credits include: *Hard Cell* (Netflix); *Halo* (Showtime / Amblin); *Hollyoaks* (Lime Pictures for Channel 4); *Father Brown, Doctors, Hetty Feather, Doctors, Waking the Dead* (BBC), *Colditz* (Granada).

CREATIVES

KATHERINE CHANDLER | WRITER

Katherine is an award-winning Welsh writer working in theatre, film, radio and television.

Twice a finalist for the prestigious Susan Smith Blackburn prize with her plays *Before it Rains* and *Parallel Lines*. Katherine was awarded the judges prize in the Bruntwood prize for playwriting for her play *Bird*. *Bird* was co-produced by Manchester Royal Exchange and Sherman Theatre and received critical acclaim. Her previous Theatr Clwyd play *Thick as Thieves* was co-produced with Clean Break Theatre with whom she has a long established relationship.

Katherine was the inaugural winner of the BBC and National Theatre Wales, Wales Drama Award and has worked a number of times with both companies. BBC iPlayer released Katherine's first film, *Tag*, as part of the BBC3/BBC iPlayer drama launch. She has worked with BBC Drama on both *EastEnders* and *Casualty* and was a series writer on the award winning BBC4 radio drama *Tracks*.

Currently Katherine is working with companies such as The National Theatre, National Theatre Wales, Birmingham Rep and BBC Drama.

FRANCESCA GOODRIDGE | DIRECTOR

Francesca is a Welsh, working class, theatre director and one of the first recipients of the Carne Traineeship for Directors in Wales at Theatr Clwyd. She grew up in Swansea and trained at The Liverpool Institute for Performing Arts. She is also the former Trainee Director of The Other Room Theatre in Cardiff. She recently co-founded The Far Away Plays – an online play reading company that champions Welsh and Wales based creatives – with a view to revisit existing Welsh plays and discuss the reimagining of those classics for today.

Francesca has been a visiting director at The Royal Conservatoire of Scotland, LIPA, Royal Welsh College of Music and Drama and Mountview Academy of Theatre Arts.

Her recent Christmas production of *Cinderella* at The Barn Theatre, Cirencester, was favoured as one of the 'best family Christmas shows to see' by The Observer.

Directing Credits include: *Carousel* (Mountview); *The Brothers Grimm presents Cinderella* (The Barn Theatre); *Once Upon A Christmas* (co-directed by Tamara Harvey, Theatr Clwyd); *REVOLT. SHE SAID. REVOLT AGAIN*, *Philistines*, *Posh* (Liverpool institute for Performing Arts; *The Future* (National Youth Theatre of Wales); *The Crocodile* (Cornerstone Theatre); *Bark! The Musical* (Edinburgh Fringe); *Adam Eve & Steve* (The Kings Head Theatre); *Shout! The Mod Musical* (Royal Court Theatre, Liverpool).

She has been associate and/or assistant director on over ten productions and co-productions with Theatr Clwyd. Chosen assistant director credits include: *Isla*, *Milky Peaks*, *For The Grace of You Go I*, *Pavillion*.

Francesca is currently co-developing two musicals: *Miss Wales* and *Without You – Badfinger The Musical*.

She is incredibly honoured to be directing *A Pretty Shitty Love* at Theatr Clwyd. It is a theatre that has been a huge champion for her development as a director and she will be forever grateful to Tamara Harvey, Philip and Christine Carne for all of their love, guidance, continued support and trust. This story is particularly special to Francesca as it is inspired by a member of her family. She is incredibly proud to be part of a family of such strong, awe inspiring women

LULU TAM | DESIGNER
Lulu Tam is a scenographer who likes to explore materials, body, space in performance. She works nationally and internationally and has been actively engaged her works in renown festivals, Prague Quadrennial of Performance Design and Space 2011&2019, London Art Biennale 2015 etc. She was a finalist of Linbury Prize and the winner of Taking the Stage supported by British Council Ukraine in 2015, furthermore, she was a selected designer at World Stage Design 2017, Taipei. She is now a visiting professional at the Central School of Speech and Drama

JESS BERNBERG | LIGHTING DESIGNER
Jess is a London-based lighting designer. Whilst living a largely urban professional existence, Jess is a proud campaigner for the environment and aims to make work that is both socially conscious and ecologically engaged. She is currently making work with Chichester Festival Theatre and The Javaad Alipoor Company, and recent credits include: *The Climbers* (Theatre By The Lake); *Glee & Me* (Manchester Royal Exchange); *Gulliver's Travels* (Unicorn Theatre); *Once Upon A Time in Nazi Occupied Tunisia* (Almeida Theatre); *Buggy Baby* (The Yard).

ALEXANDRA FAYE BRAITHWAITE | COMPOSER AND SOUND DESIGNER

Alexandra Faye Braithwaite is a sound designer and composer. For Theatr Clwyd: *Once Upon a Christmas & A Christmas Carol.* Recent theatre credits include: *Anna Karenina* (Sheffield Crucible); *Purple Snow Flakes and Titty Wanks* (Royal Court/Abbey Theatre); *Kes* (Theatre by the Lake/Bolton Octagon); *Wuthering Heights, Light Falls* (Royal Exchange); *Shining City* (Stratford Theatre Royal); *Groan Ups* (Vaudeville Theatre); *Home I'm Darling* (Stephen Joseph/ Bolton Octagon/Theatre by the Lake); *The Audience, The Remains of Maisie Duggan, Room* (Abbey Theatre); *Toast* (The Other Palace/ Lowry Theatre/Traverse Theatre); *Hamlet, Talking Heads, Rudolph* (Leeds Playhouse); *Things of Dry Hours* (Young Vic); *Cougar, Dealing with Clair, The Rolling Stone* (Orange Tree Theatre); *Romeo and Juliet* (China Plate); *Acceptance* (Hampstead Downstairs); *Operation Crucible, Chicken Soup* (Sheffield Crucible Studio); and *Dublin Carol* (Sherman Theatre).

LIBBY WARD | VIDEO DESIGNER

Libby trained at Guildford School of Acting and, early on, developed a passion for using live video and animation to enhance and add movement to performance. She is a curious and innovative designer often looking to push the boundaries of conventional ideas.

Though having reduced work during the pandemic, she completed some studio design experiments alongside being Associate Video Designer to Nina Dunn on *Extinct* in June 2021. Her recent designs include *There May Be A Castle* at The Little Angel Theatre as well as acting as animator on *Bonnie and Clyde* (Arts Theatre). In order to greater improve her knowledge of video systems, she has also completed a two and half month contract at the National Theatre, working as a video technician on *Small Island* in the Olivier Theatre.

YANDASS NDLOVU | MOVEMENT DIRECTOR

Founder of I M Pact Collective. Current Manchester International Festival Creative Fellow. First Class BA Hons Dance and Performance at the Arden School of Theatre (2019).

Acting credits include: *Electric Rosary, Macbeth, Our Town, Nothing* (Royal Exchange Theatre, Manchester); *Birth: Orchid & Syria* (World Health Organisation, Geneva); *Negging* (Bristol Old Vic); *Dead Certain* (Hopemill Theatre).

Dance credits include: *Alphabus* (Manchester International festival); *FlexN Manchester* (Old Granada Studios); *Flexn Young Identity* (Contact

Theatre); *Boy Blue Elevate* (HOME THEATRE); *Festival Number 6* (Portmeirion); Through The Eye-Rachel Chinouriri.

Short film and television credits include: *Icaria* (Nowness and MIF); *Yandass.mov* (Random Acts, Channel 4); *The X Factor* (dancer ITV); *Run Boy Run* & *Yandass.mov* (Channel 4, Random Acts); *Freestyle* (BFI).

Movement directing & choreographing credits include: *Bloody Elle* (Royal Exchange Theatre); *Everything All Of The* (Contact Theatre); *Cryptomnesia* (Future Ventures & ACE); *[M]others* (Co:lab- Royal Exchange Theatre); *See Me After* (HOME theatre); *Run Boy Run* & *Yandass.mov* (Channel 4, Random Acts).

Assisting credits include: *Breathe 2* (Manchester International Festival); *The Space Between Us* (Royal Exchange Theatre).

I M Pact credits include: *LETS GO* - supported by The Lowry, HOME, The Portico Library, Contact, Opera House , Manchester, International Anthony Burgess Foundation, Manchester Museum, Royal Exchange Theatre; *All I Want For Christmas* (Royal Exchange Theatre x I M Pact); *QueerContact* (Contact Theatre).

POLLY JERROLD | CASTING DIRECTOR
Theatre credits include: *Paradise Now!* (Bush Theatre); *Antigone, Peter Pan, A Tale of Two Cities, Oliver Twist, To Kill A Mockingbird* tour, *Running Wild* tour (Regent's Park Open Air Theatre); *Chasing Hares, The Secretaries* (Young Vic); *First Touch* (Nottingham Playhouse); *Life of Pi* (Sheffield Theatres & West End); *Waldo's* (Extraordinary Bodies/Bristol Old Vic); *A Pretty Shitty Love, Milky Peaks, Celebrated Virgins, Curtain Up* and *For The Grace Of You Go I* (Theatr Clwyd); *Shandyland* (Northern Stage); *One Flew Over the Cuckoo's Nest, Tribes* (Sheffield Theatres); *Our Lady of Kibeho, Soul, Merlin, Peter And The Starcatcher* (Royal & Derngate); *Two Trains Running* (ETT and Royal & Derngate); *Approaching Empty* (Kiln, Tamasha & Live Theatre); *The Lovely Bones* (Royal & Derngate, Birmingham Rep and Northern Stage); *All's Well that Ends Well* (Shakespeare's Globe); *The Caretaker* (Bristol Old Vic); *The Government Inspector, Tommy, Our Country's Good* (Ramps on the Moon); *The Island Nation* (Arcola); *Brideshead Revisited, A View from the Bridge, Sherlock* (York Theatre Royal); *Anita & Me, Peter Pan, Of Mice and Men, A Christmas Carol, 101 Dalmatians, What Shadows, Folk, Winnie And Wilbur, Back Down, Feed the Beast, I Knew You* (Birmingham Rep); *The Kitchen Sink, Educating Rita* (Hull Truck Theatre); *Sweet Charity, Wit, The Ghost Train* and *Little Shop of Horrors* (Royal Exchange Theatre).

Theatr Clwyd

The award-winning Theatr Clwyd is Wales' biggest producing theatre. Since 1976 Theatr Clwyd has created exceptional theatre from its home in Flintshire, North Wales. Driven by the vision and dynamism of award-winning Artistic Director Tamara Harvey and Executive Director Liam Evans-Ford, Theatr Clwyd pushes theatrical boundaries creating world-class productions.

In 2021 Theatr Clwyd was named as The Stage's *Regional Theatre Of The Year*. Major recent successes have included co-producing *Home, I'm Darling* with the National Theatre, which won Best New Comedy at the Olivier Awards and was nominated in five categories, the UK Theatre Award-winning musical *The Assassination of Katie Hopkins*, the site-specific, immersive *Great Gatsby*, Menier Chocolate Factory co-production of *Orpheus Descending* and the world premiere of new musical, *Milky Peaks*.

Theatr Clwyd is one of only four theatres in the UK to build sets and props, make costumes and paint scenery in-house. Their impressive team of workshop, wardrobe and scenic artists, props makers and technicians ensure the skills vital to a vibrant theatre industry are nurtured right in the heart of Wales, developing the theatre makers of the future. In addition to this, Theatr Clwyd hosts an artist development programme, trainee technicians' scheme and an eighteen-month traineeship for directors, to develop the Artistic Directors of the future.

Theatr Clwyd works in the community across all art forms and is recognised as a cultural leader for its cross generational theatre groups, work in youth justice and diverse programme of arts, health and wellbeing. Award-winning Community Engagement projects include *Arts from the Armchair*, in partnership with Betsi Cadwaladr University Health Board, which uses theatrical making skills to help people with early onset memory loss and their carers, and *Justice In A Day*, working in schools and the law courts to help at risk children to realise the consequences of crime.

Theatr Clwyd has completed the public consultation period for a major Capital Redevelopment Project which will reimagine the theatre's public spaces and create a greener, more efficient and sustainable building where world-class art can thrive and social action is rooted for generations to come.

During the Covid-19 pandemic the theatre has been active in helping its community, from hosting blood donation sessions and distributing food to vulnerable families to creating digital dance workshops for those with Parkinsons and sharing creative packages and activities with those most isolated.

THANK YOU

Thank you to all the teams at Theatr Clwyd.

Thank you to all the funders and supporters of Theatr Clwyd.

The Carne Trust has been instrumental in creating the Theatr Clwyd Carne Traineeship for Directors in Wales. Francesca Goodridge, director of *A Pretty Shitty Love*, was one of the first two participants of the scheme.

Thank you to Shan Cornelius Gwilliam, Wendy Goodridge, Marillier & Hester Evans, Crayg Ward, Georgia Henshaw, Kristian Phillips, Gwawr Loader and Scott Arthur.

THE
CARNE TRUST
Supporting young talent in the performing arts

Cyngor Celfyddydau Cymru
Arts Council of Wales

Cymru
Wales

CYNGOR
Sir y Fflint
Flintshire
COUNTY COUNCIL

Noddir gan
Lywodraeth Cymru
Sponsored by
Welsh Government

CHARACTERS

HAYLEY
CARL

Pre recorded characters:
PRISON OFFICER
PRISON VOICEMAIL
CARL VOICEMAIL
HAYLEY VOICEMAIL
STACEY
MAM

SETTING
Swansea, South Wales

TIME
2016

AUTHOR'S NOTES

Although this story is inspired by a true-life story, the play is a work of fiction.

Francesca Goodridge (director) and myself spent time with Stacey Gwilliam and committed to a thorough research and development process before taking on Stacey's story.

We are deeply saddened that Stacey is no longer with us to have continued the journey to production. During the process we hold Stacey and her family in our thoughts.

PRODUCTION NOTES

The play organically separates into sections. Buried, monologues, letters, strikes and buried.

We wanted to work collaboratively with our creative team in the 'Buried' sections to achieve a sensory experience. We didn't want these sections to be dialogue heavy. Stacey's actual words and how she described being buried are used throughout these sections.

I felt the monologues section were the most in control the play should be. Things are okay for both characters at this point, life is okay. We wanted this to be an easy watch and enjoyable.

Everything shifts in the letters section. Either character can speak the words, which can be prerecorded or live and all is to play for theatrically. But we should feel a definite shift in the tone from beginning to end of this section.

The strikes are chaotic and creative. In contrast to the control of the first monologues. We never felt the violence/actions had to be performed and found creative ways to represent it.

Movement, sound, lighting, video and design all play significant roles in this production.

Dedicated to the memory of Stacey Gwilliam

ONE

(Buried)

Darkness.

For a while.

For a while there is nothing but dark.

Slowly we hear something.

Breathing? Breeze? Sea?

We might catch a voice.

A sound.

A laugh.

A bird.

We might catch the light.

There might be blue.

Just a flash.

There is green.

There is brown.

A flash of blue.

Laughter.

There is laughter.

Sounds.

There are sounds, louder now.

Birdsong.

There are birds, definitely birds.

Footsteps.

There are footsteps, moving away.

Don't go.

Grabs.

Reaches.

Grabs.

Breathe.

Breathe.

Breathe.

A huge intake of breath. Louder than a gasp. Bigger than a gulp. A breath for life.

She breathes.

In.

Out.

Breathes.

Takes her time.

And we find we're no longer in the dark.

She breathes.

In.

Out.

Breathes.

She finds her place.

She looks at us.

Maybe smiles at us a bit.

HAYLEY. It's difficult to know where to start.

(She looks at us.)

(Takes us in.)

I know

(Looks at someone in the audience.)

Let's go back.

(Someone else.)

Lets go back to the day my Dad took me to the lake.

(Takes a breath.)

Lets do that.

*(Maybe there's an echo of sound from before –
Breathing? Breeze? Sea?)*

It was summer
There was heat.
And there was a lake in the middle of Wales
We lived in Swansea
We didn't have a car
And the bus only took you a bit of the way.
So we walked.
And we walked.
Me and my Dad walked into nowhere

Looking for a lake
Through fields and woods
And I kept walking with him even though I wanted to
go home.
I didn't want to disappoint him
He was already disappointed enough.
I'm nine and I don't know where we are.
All the time we're walking he's telling me to have faith
I tell him I have faith
Have faith in me, he says with a mouth that slurs
I have faith in you, I say
I say please. I remember saying please. It was important
he knew.
Please, I have faith.

  (A breeze.)

And then we're lost

  (Wind through trees.)

And it's getting dark and we're still in the thick of
nowhere

So we sit by a tree
And he says he's a fool because he wanted me to see the
lake as a life lesson and now the only life lesson to learn
is not to have faith in a stupid man
Especially a stupid man who you love
That's the worst kind of faith
And I'm the worst kind of girl if that's the kind of girl
I am
And I say well at least I've learnt something

At nine I don't mean it to be funny

But he laughs
And then we both laugh and laugh, and we're slapping
our legs, bent double with the laughter

Laughing so loud that

It hurts.
And then he tells me that the lake has a legend.
A lady who appears one day in the middle of the lake

And she walks out of the lake and marries a farmer
and the farmer is warned to treat the lady right. Not
to strike her. That if he strikes her three times she will
return to the lake leaving him with nothing
But the farmer does indeed strike her three times and
she does indeed return to the lake, leaving the farmer
with nothing
Strike one, Strike two, Strike three then you're out
That's the legend my Dad says and now he's crying
that's the lesson you need to know
I got it – that's my lesson, I got it Dad, I say
Because every now and then bad things happen.

Stupid men do bad things

And sometimes a lady walks back into the lake

And my Dad looks sadder than I've ever seen anyone
look ever

And he cries

And I ask him why he's crying

And he waits a while

Your path is worn, he says, *I can see it in you*

And then we stand up and my Dad wipes himself down
and he says, *shall we carry on?*
And I want to say no but I say yes.

Yes, I want to find the lake
I still have faith. I still have faith Dad.
I say it even though I don't
And he looks at me and he says

"Fool"

"Hayley, you're nothing but a fool"

And we go home then

And we don't find the lake.

After my Dad left us I thought about his lesson.
It came to me over the years
At first I didn't know what it meant
But then
I got to thinking it was his way of saying
Give me a chance
Everyone deserves a second chance

>   *(Maybe she silently counts three with her
>   fingers (strike one, strike two, strike three).)*

>   *(Takes it in.)*

>   *(She looks at us.)*

>   *(Smiles.)*

Okay
You got all that.
Good

>   *(Breathes deep and blows long.)*

Now let me tell you about Carl.

TWO

HAYLEY. I know who he is as soon as he walks in
He leans on the counter, digging into his pocket for change
I know Carl from before.
We all knew Carl
We all fancied him
Twenty years ago
I was in school with his brother
Carl counts his change in the palm of his hand
Al's café.
The place is a shithole.
You want a double shift today?
Al throws a tea towel over his shoulder.
"I can't," I say "prior commitments"
Al moans on about pride in work.
In his day, people were grateful for a bit of work.
Nowadays an honest days work is beneath them.
Rather take photo's of themselves and put them on the Wonderweb.
"The internet," I say.
For money, he keeps on, *only mens.*
"Fans," I say "only fans."
He sprays a table and runs a grey cloth over it.
I roll my eyes after him
Carl smiles

CARL. I know you, don't I?
"You do," I say and I ring up his order in the till
Fried bread or toast?
Sugar in the tea?

I'm sweet enough,
he says
And I giggle
Like I'm still at school
Carl Pearce
Jeans so tight I can tell you what he's got in his pockets.
I swear he walks with a theme tune.

Hayley?
He's trying to place me

Was you in school with our Paul?
I was, yeah
I'd take his brother Paul home to ours.
I always took the stray's home.

Your Mam was good to him
I hand him his change.
His fingers brush my hand.
I look up

Lock eyes with him

He bites his bottom lip

I felt it in my gut as soon as I seen him
You want red sauce or brown?

Brown. No sorry, red.

I felt it
Pulsing across Al's cafe through the greasy air between
us

Both. I want it all...
I wanted him
Both it is, I say, Be five minutes

He sits
With his back to the steaming window
Facing me
Watching me

When I was a girl I wanted to fall in love more than
anything else

I thought that was the goal

Find my prince

Cos that's what you're told

In the fairytales

Life's about love

Simple happy love

And I always wanted that

I know I sound like a twat but it's true

Never found it though

Never looked in the right place

And I looked

In the one night stands and dirty fumbles

In the pissed and the desperate

Trusting those who shouldn't be trusted

Carl stands
Plate cleared
Tummy rubbed
And he says

See you Hayley John, nice one
And I say
See me?
And he says,

You what?
And I think okay, shit or bust
So I say, will you see me specifically or was you talking
more general?
And he looks a bit confused so I push it and I say

What time?
And he says,

You what?
And I say, what time was you wanting to see me?
And he says,

Oh, I didn't mean – that sounds like a date or
something?
And I say, okay it's a date.
And he says,

You what?
And I say, what you doing tonight?
And he stands there
And I say, I'll see you at eight – in the Admiral
And I'm trying to think of something cool to follow it
with but nothing comes so the date hangs around in
the air.
And then he leaves
But he looks back in through the window at me as he
walks away.

Paul's a junkie. My brother. The worst kind of junkie.
The type you step over, grey and shivering in the
doorways of *Boots*.
The type who bring so much crap to your door you end
up
wishing they was dead to save you the shit of it all.
That kind.
I'm very clear about the rules of this flat.
From day one I say to him that if he's going to live here,
if I'm going to give him that chance – again – then he
has to
abide by my rules.
At first he does. Cos he knows I got a short fuse.
At first he's grateful.
At first he's gonna try.
At first there's a small flicker of the kid I used to know

before.

But the flicker dims quickly and a virus takes it's place.

A virus that erodes any life it comes into contact with.

A virus that abides by the rules for a while cos it knows how

to survive.

But then it goes past any conscious level of thinking and it

starts to destroy itself.

The worst thing is how selfish it makes them.

They're the only thing that matters. Fuck every one else.

That's not feeling sorry for myself that's just the way it is.

Once I asked my brother to stop the drugs.

I asked him to stop because back then there was a part of me that didn't want him to die like Mam and he said to me that what I needed to understand was that it was the drugs that was keeping him alive.

Cos without them what was the point.

He saw her die.

Our mam.

Needle in arm.

He was with her.

So you'd think, wouldn't you?

You'd think.

I did state very clearly that he's to bring no one to my home.

But now she's here again.

"Alright Carl,"

Picking her half chewed knickers out of her arse.

Jesus.

She's rough.

Generally she's rough.

But today she's excelled herself.

"Was it a late one, was it? Up the town?"

The town knows her.

The town have been there, done that.

She winks at me as the stink of her hits my nose.

"It's like I says to Paul, I might be the wrong side of thirty but I still gotta live, ain't I?"

She's up and through the ash and tabs of an overfilled ashtray, selecting her truffle.

"You given up working the doors Carl, I never sees you out?"

"We don't frequent the same establishments," I say knowing full well she don't understand words of more than two syllables.

"That girl of yours got you under lock and key, have she?"

She sucks on a bent clippy, picking debris from her tongue.

"What girl would that be now?"

She's fishing. Trying to catch the wrong fish. Using the wrong bait.

I turn on the telly. Put the volume up loud.

"You ever up the town?"

She takes me in.

Top to bottom, pausing only on my dick, she lingers there a while, unashamed, licks her lips.

"You wanna photo?"

She roars, head back and hacking,

I take the fag off her and crumple it in my fist.

"I don't want you smoking in here."

I bend into her skanky face.

"I don't want you breathing in here, you hear me"

I grab my keys off the side and check myself in the mirror.

"I want you gone by the time I'm back, tell Paul.

Both of you gone."

I run my fingers through my hair and slap on some Hugo Boss

"And if any of my stuff walks, I'll find you and I'll break every bone in your body."

HAYLEY. The Admiral froze in time somewhere in the seventies
The people who drink there weeknights still sit in the same seats
The moustaches and mullets are the same

I'm at the bar when Carl comes in the door
He hands me a tenner.

CARL. Get a round in I needs a slash.

HAYLEY. Who said romance is dead.

CARL. You what?

HAYLEY. What you having, Romeo?

>   (**CARLS** *bewildered. Who's Romeo?*)

CARL. A pint of dark and maybe some nuts?

>   (*He starts to walk to the bog. Comes back.*)

I'm Carl.

HAYLEY. Yeah, I know.

>   (*Looks at her. Doesn't get it.*)

>   (*Leaves for toilet shaking his head.*)

The only other lad under the age of fifty
Briefly fancies his chances
Approaches me
Waving a twenty and nodding to the landlord that he'll get whatever the young lady's having
He leans his elbow on the bar and turns his body to face me
Asks my name

And I'm about to tell him when Carl comes behind him
and knocks his elbow out
The lad goes down chin on the bar
Teeth through tongue and there's blood
Not a lot but enough
Nobodies sure what happened.
The landlord don't want no trouble
Carl puts his hands in the air
They stare each other out for a bit
Then Carl calls them all fuckers and we leave.
We end up at Caswell Bay
Made by the Gods. Don't let anyone tell you any
different.
Everyone talks about Wales like it's a shithole. And we
let them.
Water off a ducks back
Cos we know the truth is it's the most beautiful place
on God's earth.
Made by the Gods. Fact.
My dad would bring us here when we was kids.
He'd say
Bay born, Bay bred, when I dies I'll be Bay dead.
Look. At. It.
He breathes. In through his nose. Heavy like.
Like the world is on his shoulders.
Out through his mouth like he's letting off steam.
He's looking straight out to sea
And I look out to sea too
And we both sit there for a while
And the day is silver
Silver clouds and silver shimmer hitting a silver sea
And we sit there as the silver turns orange and purple
And the outline of the coast is black
And we smile at each other
And he puts his hand on mine.
Feels for my fingers.

Slips his fingers through mine.
This is something different
Whatever this is
It feels different
At that moment I don't know exactly what it is
I can't put my finger on it
But I feel like it's a beginning
In the silence
It feels like I know him
We're sat on the rocks, just out of sight.
I tell him
That I like what he done
In the Admiral
That he made me feel protected
And safe
And then Carl asks if he can kiss me.
And I say.
Yeah. Go on then.
And he does.
With his perfect mouth
Soft and sweet.
But it's short
And polite.
And I want more.
I want more of his lips, his tongue, his mouth
Then he asks for my number.
And I say.
Yeah, go on then.
And I give him my number.
Well, you would wouldn't you?

CARL. When the world is full of fuckery the thing that will
see you through is routine.
Repetition. Consistency. Habit.
My habit of choice is the gym. Endorphins. Keep your
mind and body clean.

Only ever been the gym.

Can't be having any time for the runners.

The state of them all red and panting down pavements, gobbing and sweating on roads people with lives gotta walk on

Wasting their time with heart rates this and pulse rates that all miles and calories and oxygen.

Truth is. Running is a pussy way to lose fat and a pussy way to boost your cardiovascular health.

And they're all at it.

Wasting their breath, wasting our air.

Mano's training all the yummies from round the bay. In their Yeezys Boosts and Nike Zooms.

Running with their trackers and Fitbits. Fit tits.

He tells them, who needs the gym when you got the streets at your disposal.

They love all that shit.

Think they're all street and down in the gutter with Mano.

He should know better. He does know better. But.

He takes their money and keeps this shut.

Your muscles need to be challenged. Pushed. Forced. Resistance.

It got me through my rehabilitation.

After she died.

Thing is they looked after Paul cos he was a kid.

But I was eighteen.

There wasn't no one.

There was a cousin. Sandra. But you only went to Sandra if there was no other way.

Because Sandra would always make you pay.

So I went to Sandra.

I wanted to stay in the flat and I wanted Paul with me. She knew a man who could help me out with some work.

So I'd go off the estate and around the big houses at the Bay looking for open cars and I'd take what I found.

And Sandra's man would take them off my hand out past the docks on the bogs.
Cash in hand.
We had an agreement and if I broke the agreement he would break my legs.
It took me six months to break the agreement.
And he did indeed break my legs.
Smashed them into pieces.
It took me a year to rehabilitate.
For the bones to slowly mould and fix.

In that year Paul turned sixteen and turned to junk.
You need a strong body.
When you're on your own it's the very least you need.

Five days after my brother goes, John from the garage knocks me up around six in the morning.
I know John from old, he looked out for my mam.
He heard they found my brother on the side of the old railway track, early hours of the morning.
They thought he was dead but he's still with us.
He's in the infirmary.
John says if I need anything to give him a shout.
For a moment I thought my brother had died.
One of many moments over the years.
During the first of these moments the adrenaline would sear through my chest and into my gut like a burning arrow but after many many moments the adrenaline knows not to bother.
The adrenaline knows to sit it out.
The adrenaline knows that the snaky twat has out witted all junkie outcomes known to man and this will be no different
Another day, another OD.
The fucker never dies.
I stretch.
Flick on the kettle.
And turn the radio on.

HAYLEY. Six.
Days.
Pass.
He don't call.
Nothing happens.
Zilch.
Not a pop.
Not a whisper
Not a nod
Nothing
For six days.
So I think.
Near miss. Close call. Lucky escape.
Cos anyway
I don't want to be waiting on a call from him.
Watching the door
Pacing the floor
I'm not going to be *that* girl.
Not any more.
I am woman
Single lady
Here I come
But then.
Six.
Days.
Later.
A phone call.

> *(Phone rings.)*

The phone call.

> *(Phone rings.)*

Yes?

CARL. Hi, it's Carl. Is that Hayley?

HAYLEY. Yes.

There's a silence then. Which I try not to fill.

> *(Silence.)*

Awkward.

And then…

CARL. Um.

HAYLEY. Yes?

CARL. I'm phoning you.

HAYLEY. Yes.

CARL. I said I would.

HAYLEY. Yes, you did.
Another silence.

CARL. I thought maybe we could hook up?

HAYLEY. Oh. Um…
… Okay?

CARL. You like sport?

HAYLEY. Um?

CARL. You wanna come and watch me train?

> *(Silence.)*

CARL. Are you still there?

HAYLEY. Yes.

> *(Silence.)*

CARL. Do you wanna come?

> *(Thinks a bit.)*

HAYLEY. Um…?
… Yes?

I go to his gym.

I've had worse dates

This is his training. He talks about being in training and his training and when I ask him what's he in training for he don't answer.

The gym is at the boxing club. A slimming world group are weighing in and Carl's training at the back of them, behind the ring.

There's Mano who was semi-professional a few years back and Straggler who trains the youth side.

Mano nods at me but says nothing.

He punches the bag with slow continuous punches.

Everybody knows Mano.

He's doing personal training for the rich women on the bay now.

Stragglers older. A small Irish guy whose face gives nothing away. He runs the garage at the back of the old railway line.

They move and talk to each other with a shorthand.

CARL. Jump rope, jump squats, push ups and plank

Your entire body has to be strong, head to toe.

Huuurrr'

HAYLEY. He tries to impress me, the daft arse.

CARL. Eight reps more. Raising the deadlift max. Another set.

Huuurrr

HAYLEY. And guess what – I am impressed.

I am very impressed indeed.

Shame on me.

CARL. A fighters body has to be able to dish out a beating but take one as well

COME ON!

HAYLEY. If he kisses his guns I swear that's me gone.

CARL. Heavier and harder, You gotta push yourself through the pain

HAYLEY. His big guns.
A glisten of sweat lines them
Like a kind of halo.
Halo guns.

CARL. In here you overcome your pain and fears and come out the other side stronger.

HAYLEY. The gym is all red and blue and white plastic.
Mano tells Carl that upping the weight on his reps might give him the definition he's looking for.
Let me tell you
Definition is already there
Definition has been and left it's mark.
Carl says nothing.
Mano thinks he's Joe Calzaghe. Like, seriously he does.
He believes his own bullshit.
Carl loads more weight, his eyes flick briefly to where I am.
I look away like I don't have a clue and over to the weighing women.
A few of them are giggling and admiring him.
I mind my business
Show him I could care less by scrolling my phone, text my Mam

CARL. Something important?
He nods at my phone

CARL. Somewhere you'd rather be?
I put my phone down

HAYLEY. I thought we was going out somewhere?

CARL. You are out

HAYLEY. Somewhere nice

He puts a towel to his face. Wipes down his hands. His
arms.

CARL. You work out?

HAYLEY. What?

CARL. Do you go to a gym?

HAYLEY. No.

CARL. You should, try this.

HAYLEY. He wants me to lift.
   I won't thanks. I say.

HAYLEY. After Dad went I stopped eating. Which was
   easy because after he went nobody really cared about
   anything so nobody noticed.
   And my sister was eating.
   She was eating for the two of us.
   And everyone thought I was the skinny one.
   Everyone wished they could be like me.
   Skin and bone.
   I ate apples and frozen peas. An apple a day keeps the
   doctor away, I thought the apple would look after me.
   Sometimes I'd eat a tomato.
   Sometimes I put tinned tomatoes on top of the frozen
   peas for juice.
   Craig next door had weights in his garage and he said I
   could use them.
   So I'd go round.
   He'd watch me lift weights and work out.
   He said because I was only twelve I needed someone to
   watch me.
   Craig was twenty-four.
   He used to feel my legs and say they were like sparrow
   legs.
   He could put his hands around the top of my thigh.
   Sparrow legs he'd say.

His hands higher and higher and then one day into my pants.

And I let him.

And then one day he said.

Sparrow legs. Which was normal.

But then he said

Just like your dad. Which wasn't normal cos nobody talked about him.

I never went back.

The ladies have finished group and are chatting their way out. Talking of having a good week and drawing a line.

He nods his chin at a couple of them, they smile back.

One of them stops

Jokes on about having fun the other night

Runs her tongue over her lip and a grin spreads over his face

He watches her out

His eyes trace her body

You know, I think I'll go, I say.

He don't say nothing.

Then he walks away, to the back room and the lockers.

And he's gone.

Turns out

This might actually be the worst date I've had

You'd think

Leaving would be an easy choice

You'd think you wouldn't see me for dust

But there's this voice in my head telling me to go after him.

And this voice is reminding me of all the shit dates with all the shit men.

This voice is reminding me that I won't find no one better.

This voice is telling me that if I leave now I'll fuck it up like I always do.

I have faith.
The locker room is empty.
I can hear the shower running.
His clothes are folded neatly on a bench. And I sit next to them.
Folded and neat like his clothes.
The shower stops and he coughs.
And he walks into the room and he's naked and he stops and looks at me.
And by the look in his eyes, I know he's going to tell me that he don't want to see me again
But he don't
He kisses me
And this time he don't ask
And I kiss him back
And it's fast
And it's rough
And it's endless
And it's not polite
And it's more than enough
And he grabs at me
And I grab at him
And in the middle of it, I open my eyes and expect to see his eyes shut.
But they're open.
And they're looking right back at me.
And he puts his hands inside my top, feels my tits.
Inside my jeans, feels my arse.
Inside my pants.
Then he stops.
He steps back.
He dresses.
Puts his kit and wet towel in a bag
I lean my back against a locker, catch my breath.

CARL. Fancy a curry?

(I nod.)

HAYLEY. And I know it then
As I follow him out
I know he has me.

CARL. Me and Mano park up outside the hospice.

Random cars come and go all day long, night too
Nothing to see here.
If you walk around the hospice and out to the back you
end up in a park that overlooks the bay.
Mano knows this place like the back of his hand. He
runs the yummies through all the nooks and crannies.
All the back lanes and shortcuts.

He points me in the direction of the house.
Six weeks in Dubai. The whole family.
Then he heads back to the car and sits tight.

This is a black and white no brainer.
In and out, smash and grab.
Fuck it I could break in and stay a while.
Make myself at home.
I pull my scarf up over my nose and pull my hat down.
I crowbar the back door
And wait for the alarm.
Four short beeps and one long one.
Like endless Mano said.
Ear shattering.
And then I got three minutes
But it doesn't come.
Which is...

This place is like a fucking hotel.
The floor shines.
Like glass.
Like it is fucking glass.
Everything is glass

And white.

This place is so white that even in the dark I can see my way around.

Three minutes

Up the stairs and turn left to the end of the hall and into the master bedroom

The dressing room is where Mano said it would be.

I pull off my hat and pull down the scarf.

Search methodically, recalling Mano's direction.

I take watches and boxes. Jewells.

Mano said the handbags.

I take what I'm told and I head back down the hall

And it's then that I notice the kid.

In the hall.

Eighteen maybe nineteen.

A big streak of nothing like Paul

Standing in the hall

Staring at me

Shaking

Head to foot

Phone to his ear

His mouth's moving

Talking to someone

Telling them I'm here.

Staring.

At me.

HAYLEY. Six. Weeks. Pass.

I know.

I go to phone him, like, a lot.

But I don't.

He fills up my thoughts

Fixed himself there

I worry that he'll change his phone

So I write a text.

Play it cool.

Hey.

Carl.
Delete.
Hey Carl, its Hayley, you felt me up at the gym and I'd like you to do it again, please.
Delete, delete, delete.
Hey Carl, it's Hayley.
I'd like to see you again maybe. If you want.
If you want.
Send.
Nothing.
So I phone him.
The line is dead and I realise that he has indeed changed his phone.
And I try very hard to push away the nagging thoughts
That he ghosted me
Even though I know that's exactly what he did.
But I can't let it be.

I get to the gym at eight p.m.
Inside it is different.
It's louder and it's faster.
Men grunt and growl.
There's no weighing ladies softening the air.
I look around and he's not there
Mano punches a bag
Eyes follow me in.
I head for Straggler, centre stage in the ring, squeezing a mop into a bleach filled bucket.
I'm looking for Carl.
"Are you police?"
What? No. I'm just Hayley. Just a person.
He swipes the mop across the ring.
"Officially,' he says 'I haven't seen him,"
He stops swiping and leans on the mop.
"What you after him for?"
I tried his phone and...
"you want to see him?"

Yes.
Yes.
I do.
I do want that
Straggler shakes his head slowly at me, jumps down from the ring.
"Okay."

Let me think.
I should have walked away then I think.
Cos I didn't know.
Why would I know?
Let me think.
Yeah. It was about a week.
About a week later
Yeah
That's when the letters started…

THREE

PRISON OFFICER. I'll take you through what's going to happen now Carl.

I'll only say it once so listen. You'll be processed through the departments and asked to read and sign some forms. We call them your compacts. Can you read Carl?

You'll be subjected to a thorough search, your clothing will be removed and you'll be asked to sit in a chair so we can check there's nothing hidden in your body.

You will be given an identity card with your prison number.

When the initial procedures are completed you'll be taken to your wing with bedding, a plastic plate, mug, cutlery and standard prison clothing.

You have the opportunity to make one phone call. In order to make more calls you will need to have money put on to your phone credit. You can stay in contact with your family and friends via prison voicemail and unlimited letter writing.

THE LETTERS

HAYLEY. *(Reads – voice over.)* Hi Hayley. It's me Carl. I'm going to tell u like it is an u can say if u want to speak to me again. I'm not one for beating rond the bush.

I done something bad and now I'm away. I got eighteen months. Nine months if I'm good an I didn't hurt no one that I promise u. Just unlucky just like me in the rong place at the rong time.

I'm not good at riting but I wanted to rite to u anyways I was going to ask if u wanted to rite back then that is good. I woud want u to do that.

When I gets credit for my phonecard then I could phone if u wants

I been thinkin about u

Been thinkin about u a lot as it goes.

(Reads – voice over.) Hi Hayley. It's me Carl. Thourt u might have rote back but u didn't and then I thourt what if you didn't evan get the letters. I said bout putting you on the prison voicemail an they said they need a letter for u wiv u signing it so they are going to send that to u for u to sign. A number is on there. Not my prisoner number. That's on here. I wos thinkin u might not want to rite. Cos I hate it too. It's on an App. They tell u wot to do.

I said u was my girlfrend.

Thing is. I don't no what to do.

I don't no.

I just

I just wants to talk to u

Thers nobody els

I think you need to know what happened to my dad.

I was thirteen when I found two envelopes in my mums knicker draw.

My dad had been gone three years.
Two envelopes
Both addressed to Mum.
There was a photo.
My dad's on a wall outside a house
People are sat on chairs in the front garden with cans.
Smiling.
There's a kid on his lap and she's pointing at the camera.
The envelopes are dated.
After he left.
On the edge of the photo.
On the wall.
Blurred.
I can just make it out.
A street sign.
Hawthorn Way.
He disappeared and we didn't know where he was.
We heard nothing.
Three years of nothing.
It took me an hour to find it.
It looked the same as in the photo but without the chairs.
But by the time I got there it was dusk.
That time of night when people put their lights on but don't close their curtains
I could see into the front room.
Clear as day.
A few kids, tumbling around.
Pyjamas.
Toys. Spewed over the floor.
Corrie was on.
There was a woman, ironing as she watched the telly.
I know it's them from the photo.
I know it's this family.
A happy family.
I've walked through the gate

Up the path
Stepping over an old scooter
A broken plastic plant pot
I've walked across the step and to the door
And I'm stood there
I'm going to knock on the door
I'm stood there...
The spill of a car light turns into the street
The rev and skid of an engine
I step aside of the door
As a car pulls up.
The door opens
And my dad falls onto the road.
A heap.
A pile.
I stand frozen for a second.
He moves. Still on the road. He moves.
Lies flat on his back and laughs.
I stand there.
Not knowing what to do.
Thirteen. I haven't seen him for three years.
The car honks loudly.
My dad rolls
Crawls to the pavement.
The car makes its exit
The door of the house opens
The woman stands there,
Fierce, armoured
She stands tall.
My dad picks and pulls himself to the wall
Tries to put a sentence together
The woman stands
Taking no prisoners
Children's faces peering through legs, around doors,
out of windows.
My dad laughs.

Makes gestures.
The woman stands
Not for turning
My dad shouts.
Raises a fist.
Spits on the floor.
Pins the woman to the wall
Threatens
Pleads
Pisses himself.
The woman stands.
She's seen it all before
She stands
Just a woman.
My dad slumps to the floor, defeated, ashamed.
Vomiting.
Cheek to the ground
Puking
Spilling from him
Down his chin onto himself.
Gagging on his own vomit.
Lying in a pool of his own fluids.
Eyes closed
Shaking
Whimpering
Shuddering
The woman stands
Behind her a teenager calls for an ambulance
There's no rush
No panic
This is routine
This is run of the mill
They've done this a million times before
The ambulance comes and I join the neighbours that
have gathered to watch.
The woman stands with the paramedics.

They ask her about her husband.
My dad.
Her husband.
I wait for the woman to correct her.
Tell them it's not her husband.
They call her your old man.
They keep saying it 'your husband, your old man'
She doesn't correct them.
Will you come with him?
No she won't
No more chances
He's on his own
The ambulance drives off
Neighbours offer her a hug, a shrug and go back to Corrie
Doors close
His wife stands on the path and watches after the ambulance.
It's just me and her now
Watching the ambulance turn left out of the estate.
I have faith in you, I whisper
The words lost in the night
The wife turns to me and half smiles
Wipes her brow
Walks into the house.
He died a few days later
Everything packed up
He had no one
They gave up on him
And he gave up

PRISON VOICEMAIL

(Prison voicemail noise – numbers – A1478BM connecting beep between –.)

(You have reached the prison voicemail service for number A14788BM, please leave your message after the beep...)

(Beep.)

CARL VOICEMAIL. Hi Hayley. It's me. Thanks for this. I wanted to say thanks. I didn't know if you would and then the screw said you signed up so I'm phoning you and this is the message.
Hi.
Um hi Hayley.
Thank you.

> *(You have reached the prison voicemail service for number A14788BM, please leave your message after the beep.)*

> *(Beep.)*

HAYLEY VOICEMAIL. I don't know what to say. Am I just talking to you cos I'm thinking people might listen in. I don't know what to say.
Hi Carl.
It's me. Hayley.

> *(You have reached the prison voicemail service for number A14788BM, please leave your message after the beep.)*

> *(Beep.)*

CARL VOICEMAIL. It was nice to hear your voice Hayls. I can't tell you how nice that was.

(You have reached the prison voicemail service for number A14788BM, please leave your message after the beep.)

(Beep.)

HAYLEY VOICEMAIL. Remember I told you last week Al might be having his knee done and I might get more shifts. Well he did and I did so,
I put flowers on the tables when he was gone. He hated it. *(She laughs.)*

(You have reached the prison voicemail service for number A14788BM, please leave your message after the beep.)

(Beep.)

CARL VOICEMAIL. Nothing much to say. Same as last week and the week before that and the week before that.

(Number A14788BM, please leave your message after the beep.)

(Beep.)

They moved me. Some scouser come into my cell trying to say he could use the telly but we was given it for the week. Anyway. He was corrected.

(You have reached the prison voicemail service for number A14788BM,)

(Beep.)

HAYLEY VOICEMAIL. I went into Matalan. Nothing there. Top Shop. Nothing. I got a new lipstick from Primark. Candy or something. Smells like sweets. I wore it to work.

(Please leave your message after the beep.)

(Beep.)

CARL VOICEMAIL. I thought you was going to put credit on my card

> *(You have reached the prison voicemail service for number A14788BM,)*

(Beep.)

Nothing to say. Something kicked off yesterday and we got half an hour outside. Nothing else happened.

> *(Number A14788BM, please leave your message after the beep.)*

(Beep.)

HAYLEY VOICEMAIL. Me and Gemma went up the town on Saturday night. The state of it up there now. We ended up at D-ream doing shots. She cracks me up tho. Off her head.

> *(Please leave your message after the beep.)*

(Beep.)

CARL VOICEMAIL. I'm not sure what you're going up the town with Gemma for. You're my girlfriend now aren't you. Isn't that what you are. We did make that official. Are you trying to do my head in? Is that what you're doing? Is it?

> *(A14788BM,)*

(Beep.)

Look. Never mind. But. Just think a bit before you. Never mind.

> *(Prison voicemail service for number A14788BM,)*

(Beep.)

HAYLEY VOICEMAIL. Straggler came in the other day did I tell you? Was asking after you.

> *(You have reached the prison voicemail service.)*

> *(Beep.)*

CARL VOICEMAIL. Stragglers keeping an eye on things for me. Our Paul's in hospital and he's clean for now. I told Straggler to check you're okay.
Send me a photo.

> *(Number A14788BM, please leave your message after the beep.)*

> *(Beep.)*

HAYLEY VOICEMAIL. I forgot to tell you my mam joined the weighing club at the gym. She goes with Sheila from the garage. I thought you'd like that. *(Laughs.)* She lost a pound. Two months she been there. *(Laughs.)*

> *(Beep.)*

CARL VOICEMAIL. I think about the gym. I think about you at the gym. Feels like years ago not a few months. You haven't sent me a photo.

> *(You have reached the prison voicemail service for number A14788BM, please leave your message after the beep.)*

> *(Beep.)*

HAYLEY VOICEMAIL. And there's a strike. So that's no buses or trains but mam said Lorraine across the road said her Terry would take me because he got a new car and he was looking for any excuse to drive it.

(Message after the beep.)

(Beep.)

CARL VOICEMAIL. Kissing you. I think about kissing you. The times I kissed you. I don't want you going in men's cars. The only man's car you come in is mine.

(Beep.)

HAYLEY VOICEMAIL. It's not a man. It's Terry. Anyway the strike's over so I'm back on the bus. I sent you a photo of me and the dog. When my hair was longer.

(Beep.)

CARL VOICEMAIL. Send me a photo of your mouth.

(Beep.)

HAYLEY VOICEMAIL. Straggler said he's been to the flat. Said to tell you it's all fine. He gave it the once over to keep it fresh. You want a photo of my mouth?

> *(You have reached the prison voicemail service for number A14788BM.)*

(Beep.)

CARL VOICEMAIL. Send me a photo of your tits. With your mouth open. I don't want you talking to Straggler unless I say. Fuck's sake.

(Beep.)

HAYLEY VOICEMAIL. I won't talk to him. Just two more months.

> *(Please leave your message after the beep.)*

(Beep.)

CARL VOICEMAIL. Keep your hair shorter till I gets out. Can't you even send a photo? Is that too much to ask?

> *(Prison voicemail service for number A14788BM.)*

> *(Beep.)*

HAYLEY VOICEMAIL. Our Joanne's got this new guy she's been seeing the last few months and he was over and calling me Harley, like Harley Quinn. And Joanne was cracking up, we was all cracking up and no one told him so that's what he's calling me.

> *(Beep.)*

CARL VOICEMAIL. Are you seriously trying to fuck with my head? Is that who you are? Someone who wants to fuck with my head? I don't want to hear about a fucking guy who's calling you Harley. Why would I want to hear that? Are you fucking him?

> *(Prison voicemail service for number A14788BM, please leave your.)*

> *(Beep.)*

HAYLEY VOICEMAIL. I sent you some more photos. I won't go to Gemma's this week. My mams not well anyway.

> *(Number A14788BM, please leave your message.)*

> *(Beep.)*

CARL VOICEMAIL. Straggler said he saw a photo of you on insta that was skanky. Loads of make-up he said. I didn't know you wore make-up like that. There are things I don't know about you. Wondered if you follow each other now. When did that happen?

> *(Beep.)*

HAYLEY VOICEMAIL. I don't wear make-up much.

 (Beep.)

CARL VOICEMAIL. I don't want you wearing make-up.

 (Beep.)

HAYLEY. I said I'd drive my Mam

 (Beep.)

CARL. She takes the piss out of you

 (Beep.)

HAYLEY. I took on more shifts

 (Beep.)

CARL. He knows you're a doormat.

 (Beep.)

HAYLEY. I might go out next week

 (Beep.)

CARL. Why would you do that? You know I don't go nowhere

 (Beep.)

HAYLEY VOICEMAIL. You'll be out soon.

 (Beep.)

I miss you

CARL VOICEMAIL. I miss you

 (Beep.)

HAYLEY. When I see you

CARL. You know something Hayls, when I first seen you

HAYLEY. When you first seen me

> *(Beep.)*

CARL. I knew it when I first seen you

> *(Beep.)*

HAYLEY. Knew what

> *(Beep.)*

CARL. I knew you'd be the death of me.

> *(Prolonged beep…)*

> *(WORDS – some Facebook posts might be scattered throughout the strikes – live along side them – a visual, throw away of words, thoughts, maybe they start in strike two – the more lost/chaotic* **HAYLEY** *becomes – it's falling words in my head starting small then becoming a jumble and chaotic – not necessarily these but examples for now…)*

I love you forever xxx,

Shitty weather, shitty day,

Love you loads, Heart and soul,

Bad day all round,

You think you have lines that no one can cross but it don't work like that,

Listen to your heart,

Happy Birthday to the biggest pain in my life,

Status – heart taken,

Things can happen soo quick and unexpectedly,

I wish it was all a bad dream,

no-one knows what's around the corner for any of us, if she just tries harder,

We had some rough patches but they are gone and in the past, our future is what's important and living it together.

You have no idea how hard it is to escape

FOUR

(Strike one.)

HAYLEY.   He's out on the Friday and I move in on the
Sunday.

We've been together exactly a year

I say move in

It's more never leave.

We kiss in the hall and we don't make it to the room.

Then we don't leave the room for two days.

I can't get enough of him and he thinks I'm a goddess.

And I am, I'm a goddess.

All hot and sex and woman.

He drives me to Mams and waits in the car when I go
in and pack some bags.

Mams crying saying it's all too fast and he's beeping
outside for me to shift my arse.

And I'm only there ten minutes tops but I know how
he feels

Ten minutes apart is ten minutes too long at this stage
of play.

When I get back to the car he pulls me in and kisses
me so hard I think he's going to shag me right there
in broad daylight in front of my mam, who's on the
doorstep with a face.

And in that moment that would have been fine by me.

Sunday night I have a dream.

I dream that I went to Caswell Bay and I walk along
the path. But it wasn't the bay like I know it.

It was a lake.

And I'm in the lake.

I hit the water and plummet down
Deep deep down
And I can't breathe
I can't breathe
And I'm trying to take a breath but it won't come.
And I'm caught in seaweed and I can see a light above the water and I want to get to it but the water wants me
It won't let me go.
I wake up screaming.
He's out of the bed

CARL. What the fuck
I say, it's me

What the fuck
He says and he picks up a bat he's got by the side of the bed
I say, it's okay,
I had a bad dream, that's all, I get them
Night terrors
Nightmares
Since my dad
It's okay I say
And he lifts the bat higher like he's going to swing for me.

What the fuck
He says and we stand there looking at each other
My hearts beating out of my chest
Cos I think he's going to use the bat on me
He doesn't, he puts it down
But he pulls my hair
Sharp
Tells me to

Calm down, go back to sleep.
Like it's normal

On Monday, I phone Al and tell him I got a water infection, and don't expect me in for a few days.

Al moans a bit, clicks his teeth and hangs up.

The dream hangs around me, you know like they do.

The weight of it sits on my shoulders.

On Wednesday the door goes and it's John from the garage.

He's surprised to see me there.

Double checks it's still Carl's flat.

It is, I say. I'm staying a bit. Carl's in the shower

John nods. Takes it in.

Says he saw Al yesterday and then he asks after my water infection.

He's heard cranberry juice can help.

I don't want John to tell me that

I tell him again that Carl's in the shower, can he call back. There's a creeping nervousness somewhere inside me.

On Thursday Carl goes out. A man about a dog.

And I go out.

To my mams.

Who doesn't know what's come of me. Not a word. Not one word in ten days. Is a text too much to ask?

I stay and help her sort out the back room.

When I get back to the flat he's pacing.

Where the fuck were you?

HAYLEY. Like a cat on a hot tin roof.
My mams.

CARL. Fuck your mams.
Fuck that bitch.
Pussy.

HAYLEY. I just went to my mams.

CARL. I don't want you at your mams

HAYLEY. She wanted to see me. I say.

CARL. Shut up

HAYLEY. He says

CARL. Just shut the fuck up.
Sit there.

HAYLEY. He pushes me down on the floor.
Not hard.
Doesn't have to be hard because something in me knows to do as I'm told.
The knock on the door stops him in his tracks.
John from the garage, telling him Paul's been seen.
And he's not in a good way.

CARL. Fucking Paul

HAYLEY. Carl says

CARL. Fucking junk, thanks for letting me know mate.

HAYLEY. The door closes behind John and Carl punches the wall.

CARL. Fucking junk.

HAYLEY. Kicks in the kitchen door.

CARL. Tell me something

HAYLEY. He's in the frame of the door

CARL. Tell me why John is asking after you?

HAYLEY. What?

CARL. You heard

HAYLEY. I don't know I say I don't know why

CARL. Tell me why that prick wants to know how my girlfriend is?

HAYLEY. He punches the frame of the door

CARL. Are you fucking John?

HAYLEY. I think I'm already crying when he comes back
into the room.

He grabs me by my hair and takes off with me down
the hall.

Knocking me into every hard surface he can on his way
to the door.

He throws me into the garden.

Kicks me in the back for fun.

He walks back into the flat and locks the door.

I don't move for a while.

Then after a bit, I pull myself to the wall of the house
and I sit.

Pull my knees up to my chin.

It's dark when the locks click and the door opens.

He sits by the side of me.

Whispers

CARL. I'm sorry.

Asks me to come back inside.

It'll never happen again he says

Once he gets back into his routine it'll all be fine

It's been a lot.

But this is it for him

I'm the one

The only one he ever wants

It's me and him forever

He'll change.

I'm so sorry.

And he is.

I can see that he is.

And I do.

I do go inside.

And he makes me a cup of tea

Toast.

Puts a blanket on me.

Kisses me

Tells me

I love you.
Kisses me

I love you so much
(Overlapping.) Look how much he loves me.
Kisses me

> *(Strike two.)*

HAYLEY. About a month ago he went back on the doors.
Which means he's out till early morning.
This is what I remember.
I remember the key turns in the door about five.
He'll be in now and to bed.
But he's not.
So I slip on a t-shirt and go into the kitchen. Get a glass of water.
He smells of beer and fags and clubs.
I sit on him. Look at his face.
He won't look me in the eye.
I remember that.
I don't want to think of where he's been.
I want him to remember what I feel like
What we feel like
What he's missing when he spends invisible hours away from me
I kiss him.
He doesn't want to be kissed.
I grab him.
Feel him
Put my hand under the band of his trousers

CARL. Don't.
He says
But I don't listen, that's my problem, I never listen
I pull off his belt
Undo his trousers

Put my hand on him
Feel him
He grabs my wrist

I said don't.
His fist is tight on my wrist
Squeezing hard
But I don't care.
I want him in me.
I want him to remember that I'm the one.
I'm his girl.
How good it is with me.
I'm marking him.
Marking my territory.
I remember thinking that.
He's still got hold of my wrist
Where've you been, I spit in his face
Slap at him
Please
Carl
We'll go to bed.
Lets go to bed
Anything
I'll take anything.
I remember saying, we'll go to bed.
He backhands me
I spit at him
I'm going to my mams

I'll kill her and you

HAYLEY. Where've you fucking been, I hear myself scream

CARL. Paul's dead

HAYLEY. He screams back

CARL. My brother's dead.
My fucking brother's dead.

HAYLEY. I want to cradle him
  Nurse him
  Fix him

CARL. Slap.
  Slap.
  Slap.

HAYLEY. Breathe.

CARL. Punch.
  Punch in the gut.

HAYLEY. Harder
  The wind taken from me.
  The air and gust leave me.
  I blow it away.

  (Blows.)

CARL. Slap.
  Punch.
  Kick.

HAYLEY. Breathe.
  Breathe
  Breathe
  He knees me
  I fall,
  I remember that
  I remember him
  Then I don't
  I don't remember then
  I'm on the floor
  I can see his feet
  Carpet tiles.
  My wrist above my head.
  Slap.
  Slap.
  Slap.

Breathe.
Punch.
Punch in the gut.
The wind taken from me.
The air and gust leave me.
I blow it away.

>   *(Blows.)*

Slap.
Punch.
Kick.
Breathe.
Breathe
Breathe

>   *(Time.)*

Twenty six days
Twenty six days of this kitchen
Twenty six days of these walls
I tried to leave and he stopped me
I tried to go and he blocked me
I stopped trying
He turns me over
Stamps on my back
He laughs
Stamps
Laughing so loud that
Stamps
It hurts.
Stamps

CARL. Lesson learnt

HAYLEY. He laughs
Out of the blue
Throws it away
Words that mean nothing to him

Mean everything to me.
He kicks me in the face
Blows me a kiss
I watch his feet leave.
This isn't us
This isn't normal
He went too far.
Walk away.
Walk away
Walk away

(Strike three.)

HAYLEY. It started ten days ago.
Two days after I went home, back with my mam.
Ten days ago I put the lead on the dog and I walk her to the fields at the back of the estate.
Ten days ago I let the dog off the lead and she runs, all surprised and free. Chasing birds and leaves and other people's dogs.
Most of her life isn't like this.
This is her best bit.
She speeds across the field.
And I follow.
And I'm calling her but she won't come.
She's away
And she knows where she's going.
And now I know where I'm going.
Faster, I follow.
Running after her
The house backs on to the field.
A grey block.
Four flats in each house.
Our flat is the top back.
His flat.
I lived there for a bit. She knows that.
She knows I was there

We're at the back of the house,
Too close.
I clip her lead back on her
And she pulls a bit a go into the yard.
But I pull her the other way.
I walk back across the field, half way across, just far
enough away and I turn to look back at the flat, just for
a while before I go back home.
I do this daily. I don't know why.
Each time I stay a little longer and I watch.
I don't like being here.
But there's this tingling in my stomach every time I do
A burst of life
About half five Mam comes through the door calling at
me to grab some bags. We put the shopping away.
I pick up my phone and delete the fifty nine notifications
on my WhatsApp and forty two missed calls.
There'll be another twenty within the hour.
I sit. Look out the window down the road. I sit.
Mam tells me she forgot sugar and could I pop down
the shop. She hands me a tenner to get us some fish
and chips on my way back. We'll share a large.
I've got the chips in one hand and the sugar in the other
and I'm passing the shop with fruit and flowers outside
and the fact that I haven't got a hand free makes me
panic more than the sight of him.
He walks round the corner at the same time as me.
There was no avoiding him.
No field between us.
I imagined seeing him lots of times.
It's all I think of.
Now here he is
And I need my hands.
He stands in my path and handles the fruit
He don't look at me as he talks
He looks at the fruit

Picks up an apple
Puts it back
Picks it up again
He's been trying to get hold of me
Puts the apple down
He wants us to talk
We have to talk
We have to talk at some point
Hayls
Hayls?
Picks it up again
At least I owe him that
Talk
I like to talk, don't I?
He loves me. He fucking loves me.
He can't do this without me.
I watch his knuckles go white over the apple
He puts it back
The chip paper is hot and damp in my hand
I look from the chips to the sugar
Trying to think of words but none come
And the feelings there
Tingling and jingling around somewhere deep in my
gut
The burst of life
He's sorry
I do know that don't I?
I do know how sorry he is?
There's no point to any of this without me.
He'll kill himself
I do know that don't I?

I don't tell Mam where I'm going.
I sit and eat the fish and chips with her and we catch
the end of the news.
I drive to the golf course and walk onto the coastal
path.

There are people down on the beach but not here
I stay on the path.
Make my way to the rocks out of sight.
Caswell bay.
I stand on the path by the edge.
I stand there for a while
I see the line of his hair, the line of him.
He's watching for me.
And he's still as I walk to him.
I can see his chest moving in and out with his breath.
What did life do to him to get him here
What did life do to me
Without saying anything he puts his hands to my neck
in such a way that you might think he's hugging me.
When I go limp enough he goes for my head.
A metal bar, maybe a golf club, I don't know.
A silver cloud
I think I see a golf club as I fall.
A silver shimmer
Hitting
As he drags me
I don't remember exactly
But I remember
I tell myself goodbye.

FIVE

(Buried)

Darkness.

For a while.

For a while there is nothing but dark.

Slowly we hear something.

Breathing? Breeze? Sea?

We might catch a voice.

A sound.

A laugh.

A bird.

We might catch the light.

There might be blue.

Just a flash.

There is green.

There is brown.

A flash of blue.

Laughter.

There is laughter.

Sounds.

There are sounds, louder now.

Birdsong.

There are birds, definitely birds.

Footsteps.

There are footsteps, moving away.

Don't go.

Grabs.

Reaches.

Grabs.

She breathes.

Breathes.

In.

Out.

Breathes.

Takes her time.

The sound of the sea.

We're still in the dark.

The sound of the sea.

She breathes.

Breathes.

In.

Out.

Breathes.

(**HAYLEY***'s heartbeat.*)

(**HAYLEY***'s voice –prerecorded – in the darkness.*)

HAYLEY/STACEY. Branches, ferns and shrubs are on me
Sand and dirt
My heart beats
The sound of the sea
Birds
Everything is slow motion
Blurs of green and brown
Trying to focus
I can't breathe
I can't move
Like I'm paralysed
I try to get my head together
What's going on around me
My heart beats
I can't move
I lie there
For a while
The sound of the sea
The sea talks to me
I scrape at the soil beneath me
The birds sing
Dig my nails into the dirt
The sea whispers
When my head gets together
I work out what's going on
I work out he strangled me
Beat me
Buried me

And now I focus I see clearly
I think about my dad
The lake
I see clearly
His lesson
Stupid men
The sea blows
Your path is worn
The sea whispers
Don't have faith
The sea breathes
I never knew what it meant
But now I do
It comes to me now
My heart beats
And still my heart beats
The birds sing
And still the birds sing
The sea whispers
And still the sea whispers
I use my nails
I turn myself
Grab at the branches
Focus
Use my nails
Claw and crawl myself out

>   *(A huge intake of breath. Louder than a gasp.*
>   *Bigger than a gulp. A breath for life.)*

>   *(Snap to light as she frees herself.)*

Onto the rocks
And the day's turned silver
Silver clouds and silver shimmer hitting a silver sea
The most beautiful place on God's earth
I crawl to the edge of the sea

Into the sea
Back to the lake

(The sea.)

Then there's shouting
And commotion
And someone's pulling me from the water
Wrapping me
Warming me
Calling for help
Help me
Help
And there's chaos around me
But I know I'm alive
I know I'm breathing
As the silver sky turns orange and purple
And the outline of the coast fades to black

(Takes it in.)

(She looks at us.)

(Smiles.)

(Facebook post from **MAM**.*)*

(In the still and the silence:)

MAM. Only a few family members know that one month ago after a vicious attack Hayley (Stacey) was rushed to Morriston hospital and was put into an induced coma with respiratory issues. We as a family were told to prepare ourselves and wait for a call as it was highly unlikely that Hayley would survive. We were later informed that Hayley had severe pneumonia in both lungs, multiple organ failure, on kidney dialysis and sepsis. A week after being in ITU a ECMO medical team from St Thomas' hospital in London travelled to

Swansea to transport her back to London as her lungs were so severely affected and to see if they could help her lungs in any way. They examined Hayley in theatre to attach her to the life respiratory machine for the journey to London. We were called to the hospital to say our goodbyes and spent several hours with Hayley then called to the family room to be informed that Hayley was too critical to move. It's been a really difficult time for us all and Hayley being Hayley just over a week ago woke up and has survived once again. She has made a miraculous recovery and we are sitting waiting outside the hospital to pick her up to go home.

(Short footage of **STACEY***.* **HAYLEY** *watches it with us...)*

(Blackout.)

The End

ABOUT THE AUTHOR

Katherine is an award-winning Welsh writer working extensively in theatre, film, radio and television.

Twice a finalist for the prestigious Susan Smith Blackburn prize with her plays *Before it Rains* and *Parallel Lines*. Katherine was awarded the judges prize in the Bruntwood prize for playwriting for her play *Bird*. *Bird* was co produced by Manchester Royal Exchange and Sherman Theatre and received critical acclaim. Katherine's other plays include *Thick As Thieves*, *Lose Yourself*, *The Silly Kings*, *Step 9*, *Peggy's Song* and *The Bankrupt Bride*.

Katherine was the inaugural winner of the BBC and National Theatre Wales, Wales Drama Award and has worked a number of times with both companies. BBC iPlayer released Katherine's first film *Tag*, in the drama launch of BBC3/BBC iPlayer. She has worked with BBC drama on both *EastEnders* and *Casualty* and was a series writer on the award winning BBC 4 radio drama *Tracks*.

Currently Katherine is working with companies such as The Royal National Theatre, National Theatre Wales, Clean Break, Birmingham Rep and BBC Drama.

Lightning Source UK Ltd.
Milton Keynes UK
UKHW021814140722
405868UK00010B/962